HEADSPACE

The Mind's Realm

HEADSPACE

The Mind's Realm

Aaron Pamei
Achingliu Kamei

Hawakal
PUBLISHERS
New Delhi | Calcutta

HAWAKAL PUBLISHERS PRIVATE LIMITED
70 B/9 Amritpuri, East of Kailash, New Delhi 65
33/1/2 K B Sarani, Mall Road, Calcutta 80

Email info@hawakal.com
Website www.hawakal.com

Cover designed by Bitan Chakraborty

First edition (paperback) September 2022

ISBN: 978-93-91431-74-7 (paperback)

Price: INR 300 | USD 15.99

To my father

AARON PAMEI

In memory of Ama and Apa, who made home a soft place to fall on

ACHINGLIU KAMEI

FOREWORD

Headspace: The Mind's Realm is a unique collection put together by a husband and wife — Aaron Pamei and Achingliu Kamei. Both are ultra-trail runners, mega marathoners, observing the world around them in an almost meditative manner, as they run the routes that other human beings traverse intent on simply putting one step in front of another, surviving the time they have to spend on earth. The Pameis are sympathetic, empathetic observers, realizing that they are as much participants in the same endeavours as others, only that they have chosen to push their bodies and their minds. The two poets are different from each other in very many subtle ways even though they write from similar experiences and seem to be in conversation with each other.

You can see that Aaron Pamei notes how other are pushed too beyond their limits of endurance, how he feels for the suffering, how he views the existential angst as a believer. He is the civil servant who feels something should be done but is overwhelmed by the situation we all find ourselves in. Life goes on; indeed, it seems too well for some even while others end their lives in despair or simply collapse and die. When you read his poetry, you remember the Covid times, the loss of lives, the despair, the long march — the poet seems to say that it has always been this way:

There is nothing new under the sun
There is only an endless circling
We live our lives with unknowing eyes
And dance life's dance with the feel of our feet.

Aaron Pamei sees the world with clarity and writes about it with lucidity and tells us that we are to blame, that we are the corrupt ones, that we are the greedy pushing humanity and this world to the edge. But, as I have said before, he is a believer, he still has hope:

I believe that the good Lord sees it all,
And on him, His perfect justice will fall
For a man's blood flows for generations
The penalty will come in one or the other

This is God's world and there is plenty to be thankful about. Not just because we have been saved from the suffering and destitution that is the lot of countless others but also because there is great pleasure in being alive, in waking up in the (extra) ordinary world we live in. Aaron Pamei has these celebratory moments but he is the poet of the city and the world seeing the disparities and power structures and the systemic devaluation of targeted human beings. He writes about the killing of an African American, he writes about massacres, he writes about political pettiness and contestations — he cannot but be true to where he comes from, to all that the people there have seen.

It is apt that his section of the book should end with a poem on the Indian flag, which ends

I only see a black band of hate
Between the saffron and the green.

Achingliu Kamei is more directly a poet of her people — the Nagas. She is also the one with literary allusions. If Aaron Pamei's work shows his love for music, Achingliu Kamei's shows her love for books. She begins with a poem on possibilities that life always holds out, the possibility of new vistas:

At the crossroads
Fragrant blooms survive
Dreaming of spring

Her poetry springs from the land, the seasons, and the hope that nature holds out. Myths and stories and history of her land and people weave her words together keeping alive the bonds that show that she belongs, that she has not forgotten. Her emotions are stirred by the passage of time, old age, by love and affection, by the blood and the violence that mark her land's recent history, by how heroically ordinary Nagas live and die. As she writes, the one thing we all can hope to accomplish in life is to, by the end:

...leave behind love and pain
Love for all creatures, respect for nature
Empathy for the weak and poor
and to have carved my name on some hearts.

Achingliu Kamei's poetry is immersed in the world of nature, the world of the Nagas who she hopes would return to it to learn to live at peace. She sees the writer as the keeper of stories, the one that keeps the fire of her civilisation alive. A life spent in rhythm with nature, to its rhythms, is a life well-spent in the eyes of this ultra-trail runner. If the only power were that of seasons, the only sounds those of nature, then the tragedies of human existence — illness, death, the passing of time — can be seen as part of the cycle of time and accepted peacefully. The lines that end her section state this with great clarity:

Take care of love and life in your generation,
...
Never forget your own insignificance,
Delusion of might and power
Cling not onto them, so desperately,
Trying to stay alive a little longer,
Learn from the morning glory,
Bloom and be gone without regret.
Whispers from Mother Earth.
I clasped to my heart the soft blooms.

These whispers for mother earth should reach everyone of us and clear our headspace. This is a volume that will speak to all of us, showcasing poetry from a couple that brings us all together.

GJV Prasad
Poet, Novelist, Translator, and former Professor of English,
Jawaharlal Nehru University

INTRODUCTION

As the season changed and the new winds blew across the land, we sat and talked as we sipped our tea. Each of us has been writing poems (mostly about the change of the season) separately, in fits and starts, over the years, getting some of them published in journals. We told ourselves it was only natural that we put our poems together in a book. Like the way we always run races together, both of us being keen runners. Hence, this book of poetry.

When the sun is sinking, and you haven't yet seen the day
When your mind is twisted in a gnarled numbing way
When you think you're too old, too wise, too dumb or too smart,
And you find yourself disagreeing with all everybody says
And talking to yourself in the mid-day heat
And staring at your dark reflection in the well
And walking sideways like a crab on the road
And the wine you're holding doesn't have a pleasing glow
And the bread you're eating is bitter and crumbly
And the game you're playing isn't letting you win
When you find their game is to just keep you playing
When you find your skies bleeding heat and crying flood
When you find your hills shorn of their hair

When you find your valleys turned into trashbag alleys
When the bearded peacock is telling the wind direction
When the snake is beginning its deep and silent swallow
And you wonder what you're doing
On this road you're going
On this branch you're hanging
On this sea you're sailing
In this scene you're acting
In this role that you're playing
In this costume you're wearing
With this load that you're pulling
With this guitar that you're strumming
With this tune that you're humming
And you're stranded deep in the dark waters of the drain
And you're perched at the edge of a precipice
And the world is looking through you and into the distance
And it's making you mad and turning you blue
And you want to be saying something that will get their goat
And it's not letting you go to sleep till the morning hours
But the words are trapped in your throat as soon as they're formed
You want to shout, but you just can't scream it
And you're scared that you might just forget it
And you're flat on your back with your hands tied behind you
You know that you need to find something else
It can't be found in the money you earn
It can't be found in the job you're in
It can't be found in the charity cause you give
It can't be found up on the dim-lit stage you play
It can't be found in the seat of an elite club
It can't be found in the rumors about you
It can't be found in the message they send
It can't be found in the noise they make

Where do you look for this lamp to be burning
Where do you look for these tears to be crying
Where do you look for this voice to be heard
Where do you look for this spirit to be lifted
Where do you look for this thought to be emptied

You'll find it in the book you're holding
You'll get it in 'Headspace.'

Contents

Aaron Pamei

Achingliu Kamei

AARON PAMEI

Aaron Pamei is a poet and a civil servant. His poems mostly deal with social and human conflict. His work has appeared in various journals and anthologies in India and abroad. He is also an Ultra-Trail runner, having participated in numerous official marathons and ultra-trail running events across India. He lives in Delhi.

HEADSPACE

I'm going out for a moonlight break
To sit down by the banks of the eastside lake,
Watch the ripples float on its face
And wait to see if they come into my headspace,
To pick the strings of my heart,
To bleed it out or break it apart.

I never had the inclination to change the game,
Nor have I ever been willing to suffer the blame,
Whatever to be had always been,
It's beyond the pale of the sacred screen,
There's no point in chasing the shadow,
The sun is already yellow, hanging low.

So let me be, leave me to my plight,
I've seen the scrambling and the flight;
The minutiae of the owner's might;
The whole thing just leaves me tired;
I'm just grateful that I am where I am
And to be here however long I can.

The songbird has set its wings down for the night,
As the bats get ready for the flight.
I look out into the gathering gloom
Is the day late or the night young?
Should I sleep with the sun or rise with the moon?
I lay down on the grass and close my eyes.

COVISCENES

'To you brave ones out there'
Says the man to the camera
As he sits down at the piano.
'Speaking words of wisdom
Let it be,' he sings.

Far out in the city, a young man
Writes, in sheer desperation,
'When it's over, please take me home.'
He reaches up to the ceiling
And ties up the knot.

Lady in the modular kitchen,
Man sets up the camera,
'This will be viral as viral goes!
Lamb chops with sage and thyme!
Who can resist it all?'

On a highway, a man shuffles
Five days, two hundred miles
'Home is only a few miles more!'
Then he drops to his knees
Never to get up again.

Sunlit porch in the morning bright
Birds set up the tune for the day
He stares at the blank page before him
'Got the whole day before me,
Let's see how it goes.'

Standing in front of the air machine
Looking down at the drained face
'You're not alone,' she says to him
As she watched him slip away,
'Lord have mercy on me!'

UNDER THE LABURNUM TREE

They had it all really worked out
The baby would lack nothing
She was six months heavy
When the world came to a stop.
Three months on, nothing moved,
The savings had all dried up.
Then she knew if they stayed
They would not stand a chance.

On a blistering afternoon
By the highway under a laburnum tree
Came was the first cry of life.
She knew she could not rest
If the little one was to live.
So two hours after the baby
She was on her feet again
She cried out to the sky
And walked another hundred miles.
Then came a rumble behind her
The wheels came to a stop
There'd been a thunder from the throne
They'd come to take them home.

THE NIGHT GARDEN

O come and see the new garden,
A season of fresh fiery flowers in bloom
Blossoming in lines aflame in the night,
Fed by bodies in a steady stream,
Watered by the river of tears,
Stoked by the free oxygen of air.
You can hear the wailing lullaby
Wafting up with the smoke into the sky.
Oh, won't you come out once
And see the new garden?

The sight will forever stay behind your eyes,
The fragrance will ever be steeped in your skin,
The memory will be etched in your brain,
Rest assured, you will always remember...

The gardener stands,
White-knuckled hands
Behind his back,
His eyes staring
Off into the distance,
Contemplating

What to grow
Next season.
Maybe he should dig
The ground
To sow in it
The other variety.

THE PRESENT STRUGGLE

The present struggles to make sense of it all,
The future seems too far to see,
The past ever tugging at the sleeve
Begging that lessons of lives lived be learnt.

Both the good and the bad stretch their hands out to be held
Even as what they are, seem hazy as the day,
They sometimes even seem interchangeable
Depending on where you are on the day.

Time doesn't know all yet on it we depend
As it steals and ticks out our lives,
The changes it brings make us stay the same
No matter how hard we believe we have moved.

There is nothing new under the sun
There is only an endless circling
We live our lives with unknowing eyes
And dance life's dance with the feel of our feet.

MAN IN A HURRY

I have seen a man in a hurry,
Who doesn't care for rules or the road,
Chasing after the high of pelf and power
Bent on building himself a tower,
From the brown envelopes beneath the table
To the mercy funds snaking their way to his stable
He spends his days poking holes and squirrelling,
As he puts on a show of straight walking;
And soon, the shifty hungry scrawny man
Has grown in girth, as does his stash,
His voice has grown louder, as does his cackle,
He walks with a swagger and has a backer,
He has a cute side dish he keeps behind the curtain,
Throws bucks at the pulpit, and now he's the saviour.
But every night, he looks in the mirror,
He sees himself for what he is—a bloodsucker,
One who denies the children their succour.
I believe that the good Lord sees it all,
And on him, His perfect justice will fall
For a man's blood flows for generations
The penalty will come in one or the other.

ONE MORNING AT THE TOWER BALCONY

The wizened old man across the other tower
Makes a three-step shuffle to turn himself around
As he makes his interminable ten-minute morning round.
Haru, the grey splattered tomcat, lies on the balcony ledge,
Whiskers glistening as the morning
Sunlight bounces off the streaks,
A gentle hum of the traffic creeps into the back of the head
As my city wakes up gently to a 40s jazz piano drift.

The lukewarm summer breeze blows to bowed sleepy buds
Promising a hot day and blustery crusty dusk,
A loaded breakfast tray lay on the red-towelled table;
The kaolin coffee pot smokes out of its pouted spout
As the BBCF cups wait expectantly to be filled.
A single cornet of a blue morning-glory gloriously
Plays its silent reveille to the beginning of a new day
Stirring my soul into wakefulness, like a feather fluff
Lifted off by the soft caress of a careless breeze.

I close my eyes and exhale in whispered gratitude.

HOBO

Asics laced,
Garmin bound,
Ears plugged,
Strava on,
I rushed
Out the door
To run down the dawn.

On the flyover
Above the train tracks
Face up
Staring
At the skies
With unseeing eyes
Lies a hobo.

Torn rags
Reveal
His nakedness,
I turn my eyes,
I look away,
Ashamed

at the sight.
Shame on me!

How long
Had he
Been circling?
Unknown,
Unseen,
Uncared,
Unsought,
Hanging on
Only on life's longing
For itself.

When he expired
It's simply over,
To be disposed of,
Like the garbage
He scrounged.

But what spirits,
What hopes
Must have fired
His life
Starting out.

What dreams
Must have sprung,
What stories
Might have been,
What flames
Might have burned.

O, You and I,
There,
But for mercy,
You and I.

HUNGRY EYES

The father woke up sweat-drenched in the dark
And looked over at the sleeping forms
His mind whirled a thousand times
He has to get them out somehow
He has done all he could to stay
But he could no longer look at their hungry eyes.

Morning came, and he was out
Searching for anyone who has a way out
Met a man who was willing
To take them for an arm and a leg
He promised he would pay with his life;
He could no longer look at their hungry eyes.

The rickety wreck creaked through the days
As relentless rays dried up the tears,
The tar stretched in an unending shimmer
As they grimly ground out two days
And nights in bouts of fever and delirium
Beseeching the skies with their hungry eyes.

Then that night brought out its starry cloak
And the super moon in yellow majesty
The dawn would bring the sights of home
Hunger and humiliation would be forgiven
They would make their world start over
Where there'll no longer be hungry eyes.

On the star-sprayed horizon, a shadow looms
Hurtling down the moonlit highway
On the wrong side, a sixteen wheeler
Behind its wheel, a drowsy maniac
The father never saw the oncoming disaster
He was whispering calm into the hungry eyes.

THE KNEE THAT KNELT

On George Floyd's Death May 2020

The neck was crushed
By the knee that knelt.
The white man knew
He wouldn't get pulled
That his friends would swear
That his act was in order
That the system is with him
As always has been
That the black needs to be pinned
Down where he's binned
Like it's always been
When the country was great
When the cornerstone was laid.

THE SWALLOW

In its dark beady eyes
They see blue diamonds,
In its whispered hiss
They hear reassurance,
In its gargantuan coil
They see true might and power,
In the pattern of its body
Mesmerizing undulations.

They clapped in unison
Welcoming the great One,
It does not hear,
It moves only to vibrations,
It slowly slithered
Into position.
It does not bare its fang,
It does not kill with poison,
It only swallows...

It began to swallow
They did not know when,
They were amaurotically swaying

To the pounding beats.
The cadence of the drums
Echoed in the cavern
Of the serpentine chapel.
Then dull and fading off
To an eerie quiet,
Smothered by constriction,
Dissolved in the gut.

What was left in the end,
Spat out by the snake,
Was a hornbill plume
And a crucifix.

THE THING THAT TURNS ON THE LIGHT

They have returned
Questions that float
Answers unfathomable
Deep in the bowel
An unease
A wish, an urge,
A want, a craving
For a click
That would turn on,
To rise again
To make sense
To build upon,
A lifting,
Is it ever feasible
Is it ever possible
That One would know
That One would find
This thing
That turns on the light
Sometimes it's on,
And when it's on
It enlivens; it's soft.

A wellbeing, a gush,
A journey, a meaning,
When it's receded—
A sigh, a droop,
A heavy dragging thing,
Is it the winning? Is it the losing?
The existing, the being?
Is it drifting, floating?

As the cosmos turns
And the wind shifts,
I wait
Bracing
For the weight to lift,
For the wings to spread
And to run again.

WHERE DO WE GO FROM HERE

Where do we go from here
This is not where we are supposed to be
The trees are without fruits
The flowers are withering in the sun
And where are the birds
They are supposed to be singing all day long
Where is this place that we have come to.

Is it that we were given the wrong map
Or is it that the directions are wrong
Have we drifted and lost our way
Is it us or is it them that have erred
This is not what it's supposed to be
Tell me who has brought us here.

The rivers are wild, and the falls steep
The clouds are grey, and the air is thick
We had started so young and strong
Believing there's gold at the end of it all
With songs in our hearts and stars in our eyes
We have traversed so very far
Tell me where do we go from here.

Now we stand at the rocky edge
Looking over at the turbulent sea
The drum beats are fading into the distance
The lure of the lutes is spilling away
The singer has stopped in the middle of the song
This is not where we are supposed to be
Tell me how do we go from here.

WINDS OF CHANGE

They said that winds of change would come,
But oh, the dust that came along with the wind!
The howling winds rattle my window frame,
The hammering of the gale keeps me awake,
My heart cannot take it anymore.

Lightning splits the sky and spits to the ground,
The dirty driving rain draws streaks on my pane
The muddy waters flow down my drain,
Thunderclaps cracks open my head
My heart cannot take it anymore.

What's the point when change decimates?
When all that's been raised have been razed,
When all that is core is thrown out of the door,
When the scales of justice have been rigged
When the arrows of truth lie rusted and buried.

My back has been whipped, torn to shreds,
My voice has been choked, silenced with threats,
My fists have been pried open to beg,
My knees have been driven to the floor
My heart cannot take it anymore.

Give me back my olden halcyon days,
Let my ship be adrift at noontide glaze,
Let me listen only to the wind of my soul,
I don't care if I'm not going anywhere,
My heart cannot take it anymore.

22921

On the murder of a leader on 22 September 2021

They feted the snake and killed the man.
It came from the sky,
It was enthroned and carried,
It came to feed the four-headed hydra,
Came to trample the freshly grown grass.
Somewhere a man walked the ragged last mile,
A man frustrated but dared to make a stand
Sang his songs of rage and defiance
But he is cut by a bullet to his name
On the road to his beloved home.
They cannot see past their screens
They cannot smell beyond their own stink
They pass their time cannibalizing
Each saying the other's tongue is different
But when the monster truck comes
Hurtling down the highway,
They are like deer in the headlights
Stricken and paralyzed.

OTING

05 Dec 2021- A massacre by the Army

On a lonely red dust road
In the broken hills a truck stands mute
Carrying on its back a load
Of broken bodies
Of young lads who after a long day
Of digging holes of coal
Were riding back to the beauty of a Sunday
And the warmth of home.

Slaughtered in the cold evening,
Cut down by the cruel fingers
Of those who crave the land
But do not love its people,
Armed with orders to kill
In the name of a nation
That seeks to pick and choose
To lift some only and trample on others.

The wounds cannot be nursed
The scars will never heal
Trust cannot be rebuilt
History cannot hide
Memories will not be erased
Graves will not be silent
Hearts will not forgive.

A NOOGIE

How is it that you don't see what is in front of you?
You keep sliding back to where you had been
Keep talking the way you always want to
Nobody is listening to you now.

You open the gates to that lonely highway
Where only you can travel on
There's no point looking behind
No one is following you.

Give yourself back whatever you owed
All the time and the money you had
Someone's stolen all your gifts and voice
Nobody is paying you back.
Stamp out the colours you have in your eyes
It is all a world of black and white
Blow away all the smoke from your hair
Nobody is smelling you up.

Where is the pair of boots you've been wearing
The ones you wore to climb the cliffs
I have heard the sound of one hitting the floor
I'm waiting for the other to drop.

Go get the magicians you have hidden in the back
Tell them to rustle up the scream
There's nothing here that's moving
Except the shadows of the night.

Singing swallows swing in the evening sky
The gathering gloom pays them no heed
There's always more in the kitchen
Nights can easily be made.

So sing your songs of elevated grace
Take the thunder and the storm
Burn them together in the singing alchemy bowl
Give them something to howl.

I don't care what you really think
It's just all there in the tank
You just dip the brush in the paint
And splash up whatever comes out of it.

THE RED-STONED TOWER

The red stoned tower just stands there
Mute. Unfeeling. Unmoved.
It will stand there till it dies,
Till the sands between the stones
Bled to the ground and turned to mud
And the colossus became a pile of rubble.
For now, it doesn't care for the rain or the sun
It will neither hear nor cry,
But will stand with its shadow over the land.
Some say, 'We will blow horns on its rampart!'
Others say, 'There's death and decay on its dark side.'
As the battle rages between the rabbit and the duck,
The wheels turn inexorably in the rut.
But the wind will blow, and the rain will fall,
Ozymandias will be reclaimed by the sands
Of time, from whence it came.

THE CHILL OF THE SHADOWS

I feel the chill of the shadows
Of the winged horse that sprung
From the neck of the beheaded one.
I feel my voice die in my throat
And hear my silent scream echo into the night.

I speak into the chamber of my skull
Where there's no murmur of dissent
I look at the mirror and weep
At sunken eyes and flailing arms
Garbed in fine muslin of Pishacha.

I see the book lying open in the marketplace
Crying out to passersby
But they only dig with their flaming spades
For the treasures that lay buried
Long turned into scavenging worms.

I hear the wind howling in terror
Of the coming night of long knives
When the grotesques unmask their faces
And the mad, salivating to bovine faeces,
Burn their own house down to the ground.

THE PRECARIAT

He sleeps precariously on the saddle of the rickshaw
Head resting on a green-checked rag
On the seat of the tricycle
Scrawny legs in full stretch
Heels on the middle of the handlebar
Few weakly blinking stars pierce
Through the muggy night sky
The garish light of the streetlamp high on the pole
Hits the left side of his sweat-shined face.
He closes his eyes, and in a split
His mind slips back in time
He remembers the stridulating sounds of crickets rising
From the waving greens of fresh paddy fields
Frogs splashing into the muddy water in fright
As he walks bare feet around the field with a catapult
Whistling a tune off a favorite movie hit.
Till one day, the tap near the field would no longer run
Till the green fields turned to crumbly cakes of mud
The village became a ramshackle ruin
An empty bowl of dust.
Thus began the hell journey of the Indian precariat.

From the brick kilns of Gorakhpur
To the godowns of Surat factories
Whatever load the back could take
However small the hours would make,
Till one day, after riding overnight
In the dark cavernous back of a rice-sacked truck
He scrambled out dazed and stumbling
Into the hot capital morn.
He trudged around empty-bellied in the blazing heat
Looking for work
Only to become an invisible stench in the corner
A rag in the sewer
But the flame behind his eyes refused to go out
And now he sleeps precariously
On the saddle of the rickshaw.

THE TIME IS NOW, IT'S FOR EVERYTHING

Bring them all in, let the bells ring
Feed the black wolf, loop the bowstring
The grosteque beast is not going away
There's no time to lose, not even a day.

We've read his mind, we've seen his soul
Looked into the abyss most foul
Stench of lies swirls in the cesspool
He rides on the back of myotic fools

Now your hunger, it's kept you in chains
You are free, but you cry in pain
Let the blind man in, he knows the way in the dark
Let him take aim, he will set the spark.

Let conscience sing, let the unease begin
Beat the drums, bring the canons in
Forget the seasons and the slow changes they bring
The time is now, it's for everything.

THE FLAG

The tricolor flutters in the morning breeze
Against the grey of autumn sky,
Bands of orange, white and green
Each with meaning of great import
We were taught early in our lives—
Orange for strength, Green for growth,
White for peace and truth to thrive
I ruminate upon this great averment
But I fail to see the white band in the middle
I only see a black band of hate
Between the saffron and the green.

ACHINGLIU KAMEI

A short story writer, poet, and ultra-runner, **Achingliu Kamei**, Associate Professor, teaches Literature at DU. She has published *Naga Tales, Dawn* (2017), *Songs of Raengdailu* (2021), and *Liangtuang Pu*, (2021). Her works were published in several journals and anthologies in the USA, Canada, Singapore, and India. She is also a passionate Ultra-Trail runner, having participated in many ultra-trail running events across India.

CROSSROADS

As I stand waiting for my ride
The ride of another tide
Crossing the life of a bride
Dreaming of a life unbridled with strife
Strife that surely visits the old, the young
It's thrilling to be at the crossroads
Seeing the old and the young
The new and the old
The fast and the slow
The lovely and the ugly
The innocent and the guilty
Flowing, running, ever moving
Trains, rivers, blue skies, sands
Crossing each other
For a millisecond, becoming the other
Till each goes their way
Life...

At the crossroads
Fragrant blooms survive
Dreaming of spring

THE MOON OF MY HOMETOWN

The full moon over my hometown
Is round, full, and pure white as the mists
It hangs above. Inviting
The lovers thought of each other,
The soft light reflecting the silhouettes,
From the puddle
Was brighter than Chekov's moon's glint on glass,
The women in my part of the world were,
Stronger than Murakami's moon
Silently holding all that was heaved on her,
No one could unlock their stories. Unless
The women open it up.
Lokesh, you got it the other way round,
Every night the moon reigns in her light,
So, the sun can shine its brightest.
Byron, oh Byron! Let the lovers roam late into
The moonlit night. The night is theirs.
Pale and weary she's not mighty Shelley,
Solitary, the trait of the strong
Emily, yes, you are right. The universe her shoes
The full moon of my hometown
Shines the brightest.

THE GREEN TALIAM

The Green Bamboo Raft

Turned another fast corner
Spun twice, and the knots came undone
The green *taliam*
Fought to survive
Looked on by an indifferent sky
A Strong squall pushed the raft
Downriver towards the fall
Frightened frogs, fish, and snakes
Looked up at the shadow above
Expecting the poisoned juices
To be stunned, yet one more time
The indigenous vine
Useful for fishing
The green *taliam*, a shadow of its
Former self
Crashed onto the stony shore
Dizzy and dazed from near death
Collapsed beside the tangled roots.

It was woken by the night breeze,
On realization

It struggled to free itself
Little knowing the present abode
Is a restful nook
Away from the gazing stars
Near the obsidian, smooth and calm
The green *taliam*, repaired,
Pushed out again, with its might
For one last journey
To freedom,
Drinking deeply from ancient cups
Calling to the river spirits
To carry it till it finds solid ground.

CHAKAAN, AUTUMN

Chakan kagangaimei, good autumn season
The season of rest from toil is here again
The *Inkhuaipuinas*, Amur falcons, have come back,
The wind is not biting cold yet
Young boys went hunting for frogs
The cattle in the fields, forgotten
Fear of scolding flung away
Carefree days, cracked lips, but hey! Who cares?
Have the paddies been brought in from the fields?
Have the seeds seasoned for the next plantation?
A happy resounding yes, yes.
The shadow of the sun is getting longer.
The nights getting longer
The fire in the hearth burning brighter
The *talums* are out
To the *inkhuaipuinas*, amur falcons' delight
The grasshoppers flocked in
Crickets had sung their songs
The cicadas made their presence felt
Through their commotion
The dogs are frisky and spoiling for a fight

The old lady and *amaipui,* the widow
Got her pile of wood ready
For the long cold winter, bereft of companion
Her yams piled up against the wall for hard days
The barn is half full of 'green gifts' from neighbours
Dailong-haeng, poinsettias blooming
Brightly on *taupungs*
The red colour stands out
Against the mountain silhouette
The earth was soft and moist and ready to receive
The earthworms and the insects did their jobs
The *bizik,* and yam
All planted in green rows against the walls
The *gankareih*, spine gourd vines left 'un-weeded.'
To curl upwards onto the thatched roof.
Bearing flowers and fruits for delight and a humble meal
Beautiful *Chakaan* of my motherland
The whistling of the wind carried the chirping of the birds
Can you hear the hope beating in the heart?
Of another dance at the festival?
A Season that gives peace and love
And nostalgia for the ones away from the Land
The Orchids bloom high up on the branches
Too high for the young lovers to climb
Not willing to risk a fall
Young lovers' stories intertwined with that of the bloom
Of the eternal orchids
The romance between the orchid
And the bird will continue
The *Raenggan* happy to eavesdrop and keep the secrets
The bean vines could no longer wait to bloom
The cucumbers waited to be picked, ripening in the garden

Waiting to join the rows of Gourds
Already lined up in neat rows
Adorning the bamboo walls
Stay on *Chakaan*, don't go yet
The lovers are not yet ready for the winter
For the long cold nights ahead
More time is needed to prepare.

Chakaan- Autumn
Reanggan- garden gate of the village where stone steps from the valley leading up to the village gate atop the mountain.

SACRED FLOWER

Stand out
Stand up
The warmth of hope it gives
They sway down the ages
Spent solitary nights
That's the price it's willing to pay
To keep the legacy alive
To pass on the heritage
The roots to water the parched children
Bereft of knowledge
Amnesia setting in
Unable to reach their centre anymore
Perfume of the petals
The whisper of supreme silence
Tales of sacred stories of bygone past
To be heard again only by the ones who seek
Put down the mantle of I, self
Pick up the shawl woven by the community once more
Under the veils of the sacred tree, you'll find yourself
The sacred tree says,
"These are my teardrops you behold

It has turned pale by your hatred of each other
It is in memory of those souls
That could not find their way back to me."
Do we behold the sacred tree only as a timekeeper?
Walk no longer in the wilderness to find the answer.

Breath silently slipped by
The teardrop flowers
The gentle breeze
Whispered to my soul
The stories it had kept close to its bosom
In a language, I almost had forgotten
I searched in my roots for the meaning of the words
Have I, too, gone like the others?

Cheti-Bu Kaji: This tree is known as the oldest tree in the history of the Nagas. It is said that once, all the Nagas lived at Makhel. But when the population increased, all people gathered at the foot of this tree and departed to different directions for new settlements. This tree still stands as a symbol of unity and the oneness of the whole Naga tribe. When a tree branch is broken, all the Nagas observed *genna* for a day.

The *Cheti-Bu Kaji* (Sacred Wild Pear Tree) is a tree believed to be as old as the history of the Nagas. Under whose shade the Nagas lived together and where 'Paichara,' the godly woman ascended to Heaven on a thread-line, has a magical aura that blurs the boundary between the natural and the supernatural. A branch broken off the tree is accompanied by a *genna* to be observed by all the Naga tribes.

GOODBYE FOR NOW

For Gairanpou 26 July 2021

filial love
day and night by his father's side
tending, caring, loving
the teenage son
his young shoulder
stooped,
a son's grief,
to see his father wasted
what anguish, unfathomable
let love ease all the pain,
comfort in knowing
he was there,
faithful to the source
of life and pain, happiness and woe
lift the sorrow in his young heart
stem the source
from whence the grief flows
his father's blessing be upon him
the teenage son learned—
how to live and to die
what it takes to be faithful
by his father's death bed.

I WILL NOT SING AGAIN

I will not sing again till the *Shirui* is made whole again,
Till the orchids bloom again in *Raenggans*
Till the bayberry boughs are heavy with fruits again.

I will not sing the songs of Jadonnang and Gironnang again
Songs of Lubuannei nor the songs of Pongring
Songs of freedom, songs of loss, songs of passion and love.

I will not open my heart in love till the wrong is righted,
The atrocities are called out,
While the dust of horror floats, the dull thuds of bullets are still heard.

I will not sing again till the midnight call stops,
The thundering on doors and dragging away of fathers,
To be returned the following day, a battered body.

Trees recoiling, growth stunted, fearful of branching out.
I will not sing again till the mountains are healed,
Till the rivers run freely on their courses again.

I will not sing again till shoot to kill,
Ask questions later, 'law' is taken away.
Till the power stops sending its army to maim and kill.

I will not sing again till my people are healed,
I will not sing, for my garden has been blighted,
The tombstones of raped sisters languishing, justice awaited,
Tears water the flower beds.
I will not sing again.

BY THE RIVERBANK

The river holds on tightly to the body,
Refusing to give it up. The body snugly lodged in between
Two boulders on the riverbed.

The current carried him downstream.
Terrible buoyancy.
He cried out to his woman.
"I'm going ahead. Look after our children. Be strong."
The unfinished train of thoughts cut abruptly.

On the riverbank
The wife and the wildflowers, the only witnesses
The shores are now strewn with pebbles of loss and pain,
The river that giveth and taketh away
The many currents. Basketful of moonbeams
Apathy at the helm
The failure of the 'filtered down system.'

Exhausting walk every morning,
Risking life, crossing the current
Having to sit precariously,
On the raft to cross the river in spate
For lack of a bridge.

So, you say it with your body and your face—
The other eroticizes and romanticizes her life.
She—trying to survive, swimming against the current
Past the civic, political, socio-cultural river
Trying to live,
Reclaimed spaces,
The current of commodities is too strong
The materialistic river flowing past her life,
But she was not allowed to board the boat.

The power of the milieu almost flooded their house,
Practically sucking them into the swirl of corruption
She and her husband tried to live right,
Working hard for their children.
Neighbours and relatives all caught up,
In the net of easy money and easy livelihood
Fancy names to camouflage corruption,
But they stood their ground.

He could feel the current,
The universe, for a fleeting second comprehensible
He felt the body of the ocean, and the shore,
His body, the very water, the soil on the shores
His heart took it all in. His lungs as wide as the world
"Son—I felt you following me,
But I see no shore for you too,
You and I were swimming,
Endlessly, hopelessly against the currents."

The politicians and leaders don't feel guilty or ashamed,
A token of some thousand rupees wiped their slates clean,
Till next time, when another family is tossed asunder,

Unable to cross the river *Ahu*,
Literally, metaphorically.

The wife—her baskets full of fading moonbeams
Grey, the same shade as her hair
Cried desolately, inconsolably to see her husband,
Carried away by the river.

SUICIDE, THEY CALL IT
SHE SAID IT WAS TIME TO GO

Calm as the morning breeze
She stands, looking down
In the garden below
The tiny flower heads
Shivering like the fading stars
As the sun lingers and tarry
She made up her mind
They all can live without
The burden of looking after
One who lingers
Beyond her expiry date.

A crescent moon
She hangs down from it
A flame flower
On dewy grass
Her final resting place.

WILL

When I die, bury me beside my mother
Under the mahogany tree, she planted
Besides, the fishpond father dug in his youth
A peach tree to shade my brother and me
Mountain crocus on my headstone.

Anthurium for mother, sunflower for papa
Let them dance, twirl, and sway in the breeze
Place a kettle and a bamboo flute
Let it bubble and hum under the blue sky
Let the iris be my eulogist.

My coffin be of bamboo,
Let me turn to soil soon, nutrients for spring
Tombstone reads, "See you at The House."
A seat and a swing near my grave.
I loved it well. I'm at peace.

Residuary, pecuniary, specific, reversionary
I have none. I leave behind love and pain
Love for all creatures, respect for nature
Empathy for the weak and poor
I hope I've carved my name on some hearts.

CHRYSALIS

The solitude of liminal space
Between society and the individual.
Twilight and midnight
The loneliness of the subconscious
Brooding of the philosopher
The grey area holds the private and the dark
Universe swirls unbeknownst
Life in the chrysalis
Dream, unraveling secrets of life and freedom
Slumbering and getting ready
Quiescent chrysalis
Swinging softly in the breeze
Things have changed
The world has become inhabitable
Chrysalis, swing on.

LIFE LOCKED IN A TIME WARP

the tattered radio on the window sill a constant companion
for the stray water drops to fall on
the bulb hanging limp, useless without its luminance,
burned out.
Anyway, the power line had been washed to the ravine
the kitchen shelves cover broken,
the old wind passing through the bamboo wall
nothing strong standing to block it.
the network is the connection, not internet
drinking tea and munching on dried meat on a rainy day
the cane armchair,
which creaks and wiggles when you sit on it
the cats and dogs sleeping by the fire
the rooster and the chickens
in the coop outside making a racket
their life dangling on who will come to buy on a rainy day
the snake snuggled closer to the rock for comfort
the incessant raindrops fall on the fish pond
rippling and mirroring the dance of the bayberry leaves
broken like everything is but pretending we're not.

TWO MONTHS OLD

Quiet evening on the road
Memory of a
'Wedding bell ringing.'
Two moons ago
Blue notes of the morning glory
Drogon bird's visit
Blue tea on the table
Summer bride's laughter
Pink flowers—a bouquet...
A smile came to his tired face
Soot-covered, calloused hands
But honest hands
Suddenly shots rang out
Dream of life together
It withers up and melts
The chime of the funeral
Replaced the wedding bell
The love song
A dirge now, for the
Two-month-old wife.

LIFE FROM THE WILD

a hot drink from a freshly picked wild herb
a sublime gift for the body
from mother earth
hidden from the proud and haughty
spurned by the civilized
the goodness of
walking barefoot,
harvesting what for the civilized are wild weeds,
the dew, the morning drink
the civilized man told, ages ago
not food for man,
made fun of natural food
made the other look like animals
said processed food was the food
now, civilized men say
after obesity, diabetes, hypertension
carcinoma, depression
all paid their ominous visits
in quick succession—
back to natural food is the way
he said and declared he discovered
this great truth.

SOME TRAILS

Some trails are more enigmatic,
These trails absorbed the elements,
Of the people who had sojourned on it
Built-in multicolored stones of joy and sorrow,
Dotted with Neem and Gulmohar trees,
Kind and watchful laburnums
Migrants stopped to rest under their shades,
Some trails

Not a priority for strategist politicians
Wily businessmen busy on some other trails
Raging mobs have no fuel near it,
Conmen don't prey on them yet
Some trails are just right for you.

FIRE

She warms herself
It's too hot, it gives her shin bones sunspots
The other hot thing is the sun
It gave her face sunspots
She's been asked to preserve the fire
Which was once made by the master
So she has many more stories of keeping the
Fire going
So if there are stories near the fire
It's simply because
She preserves it and keeps it alive
Fire
She

DAWN BREAK

The columns of rocks, the cairns, the memorial stones
The sacred banyan tree, the sacred pear tree
The land, the river, the mountain
Hosts to a civilized way of life long since departed,
Honour, respect, covenant-making
Refined and strengthened from time immemorial
Most of it was lost by the collective efforts of the
'Great Masters', the 'Civilized Savages'
Lost in the silence of 'awakening'
From 'darkness to light' to 'modernity' and blown away.

But again, the rocks, the cairns, the trees of our ancestors
Cry out to us, loudly, clearly, forcefully, patiently
Come back to your memory of the cultural roots
Come and rest on my stones, converse again with civility
Sit down under my shade, pause a moment to think
See the sacred flower blooming again
Seek not the things offered by capitalism, materialism
Hoarding is not in your nature
Giving and sharing is your way.

Sing again of nature to nurture you and yours
The strains of the beautiful *inrah*
May it awaken the plants again, regenerate your soul
Release consumerism, selfishness,
Sing again with the ancestors
Bubbling again like the brooks, the rivulets
Call back the clouds, the rain, and the birds
Make a beautiful song

Forget how to negotiate with force—with guns
Forget the alien-savaged ways—that's not your ways
Bring back the art of negotiating
With words and understanding
The 'Civilized Savages' had you under a spell
They struggled with arms for profit, for land, for power
Leaving destruction behind every footprint of theirs
The shards of shattered culture and tradition
Pluck it off from your wounded soul
Let the ancestors' river of truth wash you clean and heal
Restoring your equilibrium.

Listen to the whispers of the autumn leaves,
Their memories are truths
Listen to the truth in your true name
Given name —invaluable stories
Not in the names given you by the 'Civilized Savages'
Your ails and ills are begotten by the alien virus and food
Your organic foodways are the best
'Modern dreams' thrust on you in a blink
Shed it. Shed it.

Listen to the song of the river stones
Come back to its fertile banks

Wash your foreign dreams away in its cool waters
The fever will finally go.

Be steady as the rock, never stop flowing like the river
Set roots deep again like the Mighty Tree
Our ancestors showed us the way; trust the trail
Hold your head high. Your ways are the civilized ways
Food for all. Land for all.
Open barns. *Lunggai-chinghkhiumei*
Compassion always accompanies riches
Chakhuang-champoumei, putting others before you
Gansu-ganthau's wisdom
Caring for fellow beings, the community stands together
When difficult times are upon them.

Look up. Stoop no more. Be ashamed no more.
Hold your head high
Wash the grime of imposed history (ies) away
And make your soul whole again
Look no longer through the lens of the 'Civilized Savages'
Shed their cloaks of lies and guiles

The Dawn is breaking.

THE FLOWER

I want to bloom in season
In the deep of the woods
Not hurried on by winds of change
Only as long as seasons permit,
Not prolonged by technology.

I want to bloom
Where mushrooms and mosses grow,
Equally loved
In the open, bright and carefree
With no need to hide.

I want to bloom
Where I'm not preyed upon
Without the need to mimic
And seed in my own time
Not forced to pollinate.

I want to bloom
Where the cameras do not capture me
Compromising my privacy

Where loss is grieved genuinely,
Then becomes soil.

Where tears become the dews
That waters to bloom—again—in another season.
In the deep of the woods
I long to bloom where my friends are.

CREATING MAGIC

Beneath the sunset sky, my lover and I,
Dwell on bed of rich green grass and moss.
Children laugh, running about, light as feathers,
In the garden, gathering fireflies.
Flashing lights, blink, hide, and reappear,
Creating magic, this warm night.
Above, the two illuminated beings,
Contemplate their very essence—
Brilliance and grace, as they cross paths.
The children dance, like the stars
Flitting and darting, reflecting mirrors.
My lover and I, contented,
Beneath the moonbeam.

FOREST

Forest mentor
I long to see my path
Thick forests hide my vision
Show me your way
River clear, reflect foliage sky
Blue ranges sing me a song
Whispering wind come to my rescue
Ancient spirits, secret tongues,
Write for me your rites
I am the daughter, I am the One
Descendant of hunters, gatherers,
The journey is waiting for me
I prepare throughout the night
My mission to find and recover
The devoured skin.
My brothers went east, west, north and south
Return them to our beginning
Ancient spirits, lend me your wisdom
Buried mysteries, open up
My hunger's fire for the trail
Not born as a son, born a daughter of the land
Seer woman's wisdom I seek
Forest mentor, show me your way,
So I can fulfill my destiny.

WIDOW

My heart my heart
Broken bangles
Red pieces around my wrists
Rainbow stars on the ground
A shroud for my love

My heart my heart
This pain is not new
Flowing hair swirling
In the dark-detached strands
Shorn, cut for my love

My heart, my heart
The last rites
Burned woods and oil
Under the waning moon
You crossed over.

WHISPERS FROM MOTHER EARTH

My heart skipped a beat to see,
As she woke with the mists.
Her sweet cheeks turned to the light,
The dream was still in her eyes.
Her fragile petals open,
Leaning on its trellis gingerly,
The warm glow of the languid winter sun
Its first rays shone on her.
Morning glories bloom, glory bound.
I caress, tingling sensations on my fingers.
Mother earth sends me her message.
I listened closely to the soft voice,
The soft throbbing cups, a medium
The faint whispers, wafting up and out,
From the petals of blue,
The message reached my eager ears.
Watch and never forget—
Take care of love and life in your generation,
Transient bloom of life, blue beauty
Never forget your own insignificance,
Delusion of might and power

Cling not onto them, so desperately,
Trying to stay alive a little longer,
Learn from the morning glory,
Bloom and be gone without regret.
Whispers from Mother Earth.
I clasped to my heart the soft blooms.

Acknowledgments

We are grateful to *Lipi Magazine*, *Setu*, *Imphal Free Press*, *Souvenirs of Best Poetry* in English, *Global Poemic*, *Winters' Ambivalence*, *People's Journal*, and *Kaleidoscope*—the journals and anthologies that published our works. We are indebted to Kiriti Sengupta and Hawakal for accepting our work for publication and for the beautiful book cover. We are deeply grateful to Prof GJV Prasad for his constant support and the foreword. Last but not the least, we thank all our friends who support and encourage us to keep writing.

www.ingramcontent.com/pod-product-compliance
Lightning Source LLC
LaVergne TN
LVHW041131150826
845673LV00007B/2267

* 9 7 8 9 3 9 1 4 3 1 7 4 7 *